St. Augustine

by Frances E. Ruffin

Reading consultant: Susan Nations, M.Ed., author/literacy coach/consultant in literacy development

Please visit our web site at: www.earlyliteracy.cc
For a free color catalog describing Weekly Reader® Early Learning Library's list of high-quality books, call 1-877-445-5824 (USA) or 1-800-387-3178 (Canada). Weekly Reader® Early Learning Library's fax: (414) 336-0164.

Library of Congress Cataloging-in-Publication Data

Ruffin, Frances E.
St. Augustine / by Frances E. Ruffin.
p. cm. — (Places in American history)
Includes bibliographical references and index.
ISBN 0-8368-6412-3 (lib. bdg.)
ISBN 0-8368-6419-0 (softcover)
1. Saint Augustine (Fla.)—History—Juvenile literature. 2. Timucua Indians—Florida—Saint Augustine—History—Juvenile literature. 3. Spaniards—Florida—Saint Augustine—History—Juvenile literature. 4. Florida—History—To 1821—Juvenile literature. I. Title.
F319.S2R84 2006
975.9'1801—dc22 2005026270

This edition first published in 2006 by
Weekly Reader® Early Learning Library
A Member of the WRC Media Family of Companies
330 West Olive Street, Suite 100
Milwaukee, WI 53212 USA

Managing Editor: Valerie J. Weber
Editor: Barbara Kiely Miller
Art direction: Tammy West
Graphic design: Dave Kowalski
Photo research: Diane Laska-Swanke

Photo credits: Cover, title, pp. 19, 21 St. Augustine, Ponte Vedra and The Beaches Visitors and Convention Bureau; pp. 4, 17 © Gibson Stock Photography; p. 5 Dave Kowalski/© Weekly Reader Early Learning Library, 2006; pp. 6, 10 © North Wind Picture Archives; pp. 7, 9 © MPI/Getty Images; pp. 8, 13, 14, 16 © Nancy Carter/North Wind Picture Archives; pp. 11, 18, 20 © James P. Rowan; p. 12 © Hulton Archive/Getty Images

Printed in the United States of America

1 2 3 4 5 6 7 8 9 10 09 08 07 06

Table of Contents

The Castillo de San Marcos fort once protected the settlement of St. Augustine.

The Nation's Oldest City

St. Augustine is a city on the eastern coast of Florida. It is the oldest city in the United States. More than four hundred years ago, it was a Spanish settlement. It is the oldest European settlement in the country.

In March 1513, Juan Ponce de León sailed to Florida from Puerto Rico, where he was the governor. This Spanish explorer landed near what is now St. Augustine. He claimed the land for the king of Spain. He hoped to discover gold and silver but found none.

This map shows Ponce de León's trip to Florida from Puerto Rico. He was the first European to explore Florida.

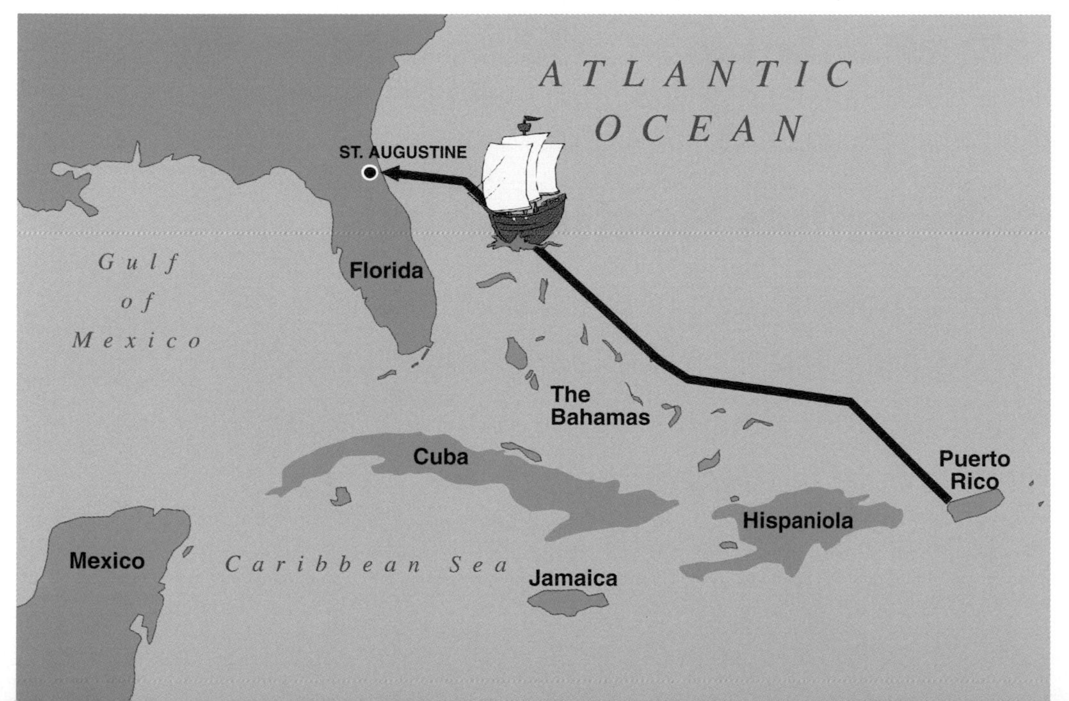

After Pedro Menéndez arrived in Florida, he planned the new settlement of St. Augustine.

A Spanish Settlement

In 1565, Spain's king sent Pedro Menéndez de Aviles to explore Florida. Menéndez came with eight hundred people. Some were soldiers. Others were farmers and their wives. They settled along the St. John's River.

Menéndez named the new settlement St. Augustine. The French had settled nearby a year earlier. Spain's king did not want the French in Florida. Soon after coming to Florida, the Spanish fought the French and captured their settlement.

French settlers who lived near St. Augustine built Fort Caroline in 1564.

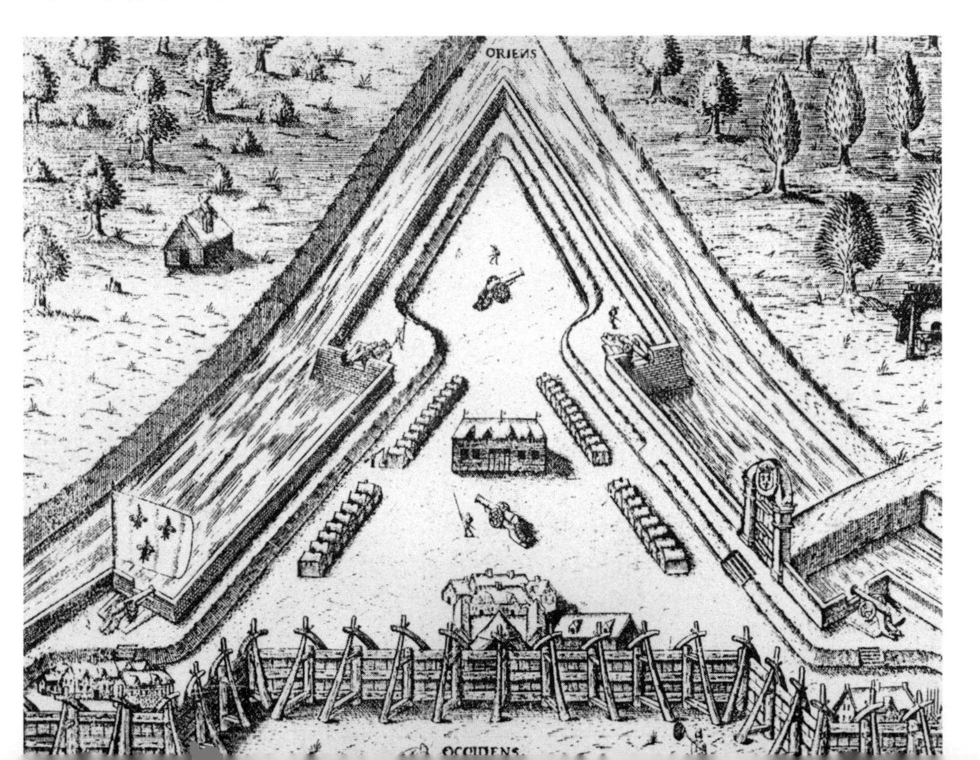

Some Timucuans built homes like this one from the long, thin leaves of palm trees.

Native Americans had lived in Florida for thousands of years. European settlers called these people the Timucuan Indians. The settlers took the Timucuan's land. They gave them illnesses. Many Indians died.

The Timucuans also attacked the Spanish settlers. The settlers soon ran out of food. They had arrived too late to plant gardens. Many settlers became sick from drinking the water.

A Spanish explorer drew this map of a Timucuan village.

A New Town

During the summer of 1566, a group of ships arrived in St. Augustine. The ships brought supplies and more than one thousand people. The new settlers built houses, planted gardens, and dug wells for fresh water. A town began to take shape.

The Spanish sailed to North America in ships called galleons.

The walls of Castillo de San Marcos were built 20 feet (6 meters) high. A water-filled ditch called a moat surrounded the fort.

The British and some Natives attacked the Spanish settlers. In 1671, the settlers began to build a new fort for protection. They named it Castillo de San Marcos. The Spanish and some Native Americans worked on the fort. Africans who lived in the colony helped, too.

Many Africans who came to St. Augustine were free people. Later, they were forced to become slaves.

Some Africans had come to St. Augustine with Spanish explorers. Others had been slaves in the British colonies north of Florida. When the slaves ran away, the Spanish gave them their freedom. In 1738, Fort Mose (pronounced "moe-SAY") was built nearby. It was the first settlement of free black people in what is now the United States.

In 1763, the British won a war. They won control of most of North America, including Florida. The British let people from many countries move to St. Augustine. It became the first American city with settlers from many countries.

This statue honors Spanish settlers who came to St. Augustine from the island of Minorca. They arrived in 1777, when the British ruled Florida.

After the Revolutionary War, Spain gained Florida again. In 1821, Spain gave Florida to the United States. In 1845, Florida became the twenty-seventh state in the nation.

The flags of Great Britain, Florida, the United States, and Spain fly over the Spanish Quarter of St. Augustine.

St. Augustine Facts: The Nation's Oldest City

St. Augustine is the first and oldest permanent settlement by Europeans in the United States.

St. Augustine was settled forty-two years before the English colony of Jamestown, Virginia. Pedro Menéndez landed at St. Augustine fifty-five years before the Pilgrims arrived at Plymouth Rock in Massachusetts.

St. Augustine had the first government in North America with European laws.

St. Augustine was the first state capital of Florida.

Fort Mose was the country's first community of free black people.

Castillo de San Marcos is the oldest fort in the United States made from stone blocks.

© Nancy Carter/North Wind Picture Archives

Flagler College was once a hotel for rich people.

Saving Old St. Augustine

For many years, St. Augustine was a quiet town. Hundreds of old Spanish buildings still stood. Then, in the 1880s, wealthy people began to visit. They liked the city's warm weather, beaches, and historic places. Henry Morrison Flagler bought land and built hotels. Most of the old buildings were torn down.

In 1935, city leaders began a program to save St. Augustine's history. The program saved thirty-six Spanish buildings. The city rebuilt old buildings. It dug up objects that belonged to the early settlers.

People called archeologists are digging up and studying objects from the earliest days of St. Augustine.

Built in 1703, this house in St. Augustine is often called "the oldest house in America."

Visiting St. Augustine

More than two million people come to St. Augustine each year. Visitors can walk down the narrow streets that the Spanish made. They can visit the Government House Museum. It was built in 1713. Gold coins from Spanish shipwrecks are on display there.

The part of the city with old, Spanish buildings is called the Spanish Quarter. Other buildings there have been rebuilt to look old. People in these buildings are dressed in colonial clothing. They show how Spanish soldiers and their families lived in the 1740s. They shoe horses and make candles. They grow gardens and build houses.

St. George Street is in the historic Spanish Quarter. This narrow street was the main street of the Spanish settlement.

At the Castillo de San Marcos, visitors can see men dressed as Spanish soldiers fire cannons.

The Castillo de San Marcos still stands. The fort took twenty-three years to build. Its walls are made from blocks of stone formed from crushed seashells. The high walls are so strong that no enemy could destroy them or capture the fort.

St. Augustine celebrates its birthday as the nation's oldest city in September. It also celebrates the birthday of founder Pedro Menéndez, its European settlers, and its Native people.

St. Augustine is a city of many firsts in North America. It is a city that remembers and honors its place in history.

Dancers wearing Spanish costumes celebrate the birthday of founder Pedro Menéndez in February.

Glossary

colony – a place that is controlled by a government in another country

explore – to travel to and search unknown or little-known places

fort – an area or building made stronger to protect against attacks. Walls usually surround forts.

Pilgrims – English settlers who founded Plymouth Colony in what is now Massachusetts

Revolutionary War – the war fought from 1775 to 1783 between Great Britain and its American colonies

settlement – a small community in a new place; an area where a group of people live together

slaves – people who are owned by other people and made to work without pay. They are not free.

For More Information

Books

Castillo De San Marcos. Famous Forts throughout American History (series). Charles W. Maynard (PowerKids Press)

Historic St. Augustine. Historic Landmarks (series). Jason Cooper (Rourke Publishing,)

Juan Ponce De León. Fact Finders Biographies (series). Marc Tyler Nobleman (Fact Finders)

Life in St. Augustine. Picture the Past (series). Sally Isaacs (Heinemann Library)

Web Sites

Castillo de San Marcos: A Virtual Tour
www.harcourtschool.com/activity/castillo/castillo.html
Tour this historic fort and learn how it was built and the names of its different parts.

Juan Ponce de Leon
www.enchantedlearning.com/explorers/page/d/deleon.shtml
Read about the first European to set foot in Florida.

Index

About the Author

Frances E. Ruffin has written more than twenty-four books for children. She enjoys reading and writing about the lives of famous and ordinary people. She lives in New York City with her son, Timothy, a young writer who is writing his first novel.